中英双语版

企鹅经典 名人大发现

查理·卓别林

[美]帕特里夏·布伦南·得穆思（Patricia Brennan Demuth）◎著 [美]格雷戈里·科普兰（Gregory Copeland）◎绘 史芷溪◎译

Who Was Charlie Chaplin?

湖南科学技术出版社 小博集 BOOKY KIDS
·长沙·

著作权合同登记号：字18-2024-194

图书在版编目（CIP）数据

名人大发现. 查理·卓别林 ：汉英对照 /（美）帕特里夏·布伦南·得穆思（Patricia Brennan Demuth）著 ；史芷溪译 ；（美）格雷戈里·科普兰（Gregory Copeland）绘. -- 长沙 ：湖南科学技术出版社，2025. 1. --（企鹅经典）. -- ISBN 978-7-5710-3267-8

Ⅰ. H319. 4

中国国家版本馆CIP数据核字第2024QB8438号

上架建议：科普读物

QI' E JINGDIAN · MINGREN DA FAXIAN：ZHONG-YING SHUANGYU BAN CHALI ZHUOBIELIN

企鹅经典·名人大发现：中英双语版　查理·卓别林

著　　者：[美] 帕特里夏·布伦南·得穆思（Patricia Brennan Demuth）
绘　　者：[美] 格雷戈里·科普兰（Gregory Copeland）
译　　者：史芷溪
出 版 人：潘晓山
责任编辑：刘　竞
策划出品：李　炜　张苗苗　文赛峰
策划编辑：马　瑄
特约编辑：杜佳美
营销编辑：付　佳　杨　朔　周晓茜
装帧设计：利　锐
内文排版：金锋工作室
出　　版：湖南科学技术出版社
（湖南省长沙市芙蓉中路416号　邮编：410008）
网　　址：www.hnstp.com
印　　刷：三河市航远印刷有限公司
经　　销：新华书店
开　　本：875 mm × 1230 mm 1/32
字　　数：103千字
印　　张：5.25
版　　次：2025年1月第1版
印　　次：2025年1月第1次印刷
书　　号：ISBN 978-7-5710-3267-8
定　　价：22.00元

若有质量问题，请致电质量监督电话：010-59096394　　团购电话：010-59320018

目 录

Contents

谁是查理·卓别林？

在20世纪初，美国各地的电影院都充满欢声笑语，这一切都是因为大银幕上一个有趣的小家伙。他身上穿的裤子和鞋子都太大了，但他的帽子和外套又太小了。他走路的时候迈着外八字，非常古怪。当他瞪大双眼，抽动他的小胡子时，观众便迫不及待地想看看他接下来又会遇到什么麻烦。这个电影角色被称为“小流浪汉”。

查理·卓别林就是这个戴着假胡子的角色的扮演者，他创造了“小流浪汉”。查理还创作、主演和导演了自己的电影。小流浪汉总是过着身无分文的失业生活，但查理本人是世界上收入最高、最著名的演员。他没有在影片中说过一句台词便得到了如此成就。

因为那是无声电影的时代，没有声音会从大银幕上发出来，当时的发明家们还没有找到为电影录音的方法，

所以演员们用手势和面部表情来表演剧情，就像玩猜谜游戏一样，在这方面没人比查理·卓别林做得更好。

尽管他的“影片生活”充满了幽默，但查理的真实生活并非如此。他在伦敦度过贫穷的童年，令人心碎。他的父亲抛弃了家庭，他的母亲由于精神崩溃而无法妥善照顾她的孩子。然而，历史却微笑着记住了查理。他是让美国人捧腹大笑的电影先驱。

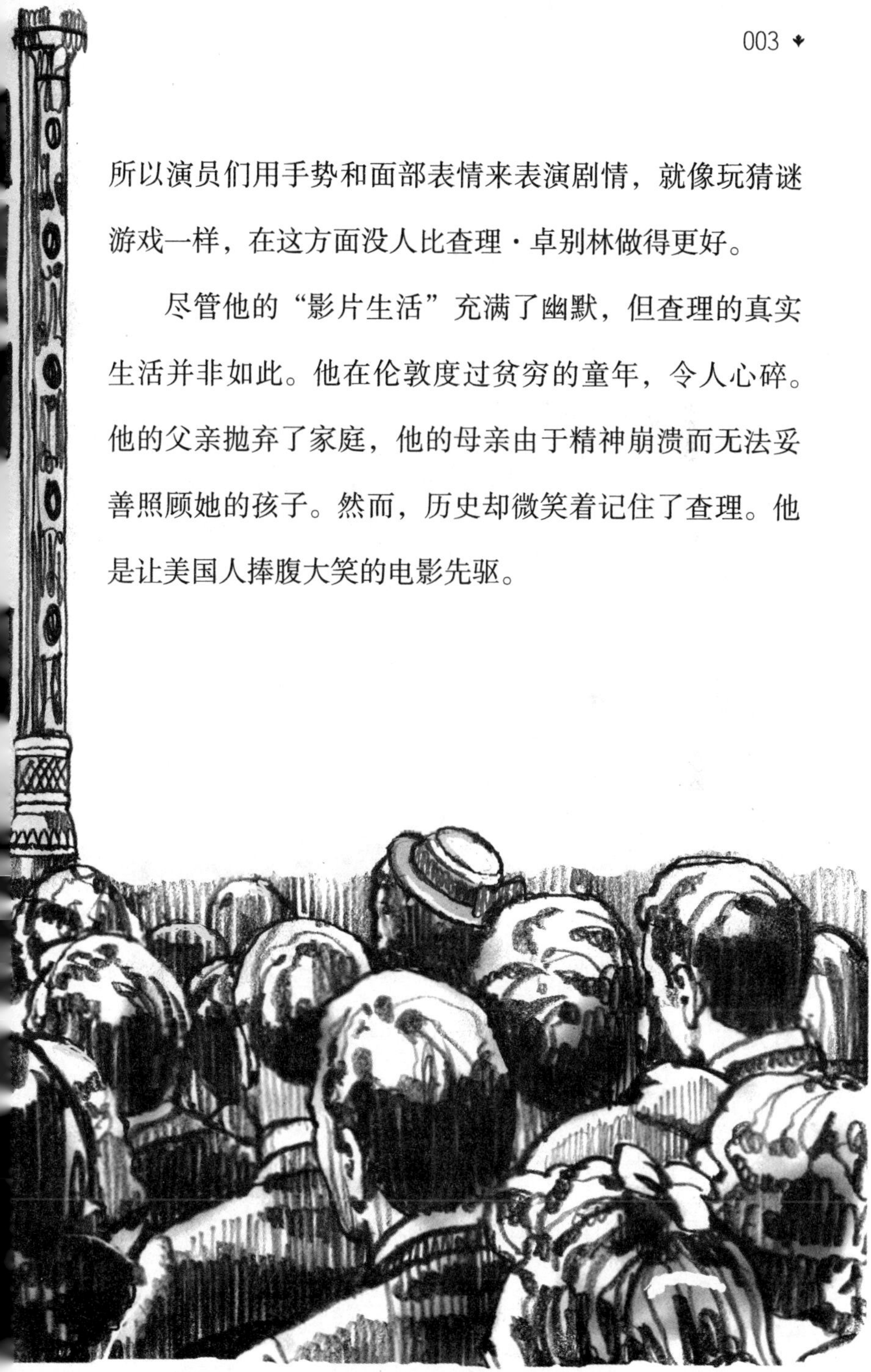

第一章

贫困的童年

美国是查理成名的地方，但是英格兰才是他的家乡。查尔斯·斯潘塞·卓别林，1889 年 4 月 16 日出生于伦敦。他同母异父的哥哥悉尼比他大四岁。

查理长大后成为一名演员并不奇怪：他的父母都是演艺人员。他们在英国的杂耍剧院演出，这些剧院以歌舞表演和喜剧表演为特色节目。他的父亲是一名成功的演员和词曲作者，他的母亲则是一名歌手。

老查尔斯·卓别林是一个随和又富有魅力的人，但他有酗酒的毛病。没有人能够长久地依靠他生活下去。当查理一岁大时，他的父亲就带着他的歌谣离开了。

查理的母亲汉娜尽了最大的努力去抚养孩子们。她身材娇小，头发长到可以坐在上面。尽管她精神抖擞地面对生活，工作却总是来了又去，因此家里的经济状况总是十分紧张。

尽管如此，这个小家庭还是有过一阵幸福的日子。当查理刚学会走路的时候，汉娜就开始教他跳舞。为了让她的儿子们开心，汉娜从她的行李箱里拿出戏服和假发，表演她心中熟记的戏剧。

有一晚，汉娜的歌唱生涯戛然而止。她的嗓音在歌

唱到一半的时候突然沙哑了。观众朝着台上的汉娜喝倒彩。手忙脚乱的经理却把小查理推到台上代替她！查理当时只有五岁，但多年来他一直在后台看表演，熟记了所有的曲目。

当这个小男孩开始唱歌跳舞时，观众变得安静了。

很快他们又笑又欢呼，然后他们把硬币扔到舞台上。查理在唱到一半的时候停了下来，到处跑去捡钱。观众因此笑得更厉害了。

查理从此大受欢迎。然而，汉娜的职业生涯结束了。她再也没有唱过歌了。“那天晚上是我第一次登台，”查

理后来写道，“也是母亲的最后一次。”

这个家庭开始变得越来越拮据。汉娜做针线活挣了一点钱，但还不够付账。她只能拆掉自己的旧衣服来给儿子们做衣服。由于经常拖欠房租，卓别林一家只好一

次又一次地搬家。他们一开始住在一套三居室的公寓里。随后，他们搬进了一所二居室的房子。最后，他们只能蜗居在有臭味的泡菜厂后面的一套一居室公寓里。

随着时间的推移，汉娜的身体变得十分虚弱，病得

杂耍剧院

杂耍剧院通常会举办一些种类繁多，令人眼花缭乱的现场表演。杂耍艺人会表演空中飞人，腹语艺人会装成假人说话，歌手和舞者则会带来歌舞表演。那里还有表演高空走钢索的人、驯兽师和表演杂技转碟的人。

美国也有杂耍剧院。杂耍表演最辉煌的时期是20世纪初。当电影流行起来时，英国和美国的杂耍剧院就逐渐退出了历史的舞台。

无法再支撑下去了。她只好领着儿子们去了济贫院，那里是伦敦的穷人走投无路时的最后一个去处。

这个小家庭就此被拆散了。汉娜被送进了疗养院，这是一个为那些病得无法在济贫院谋生的人准备的地方。查理和悉尼被带到一所名为汉韦尔的孤儿学校。查理紧紧地抱着他的哥哥，但悉尼不得不和年长一些的男孩待

英国济贫院

在查理的童年时期，那些负担不起生活开销的穷人会被送到济贫院。如果有能力的话，他们会在那里用劳动来换取自己的住所和食物。一家人会被分开，每天只能见一次面。每个人都穿着制服，睡的是大通铺，坐在大食堂的长椅上吃饭。没人想沦落到济贫院中。然而，它或许拯救了许多在街头挨饿的人。

汉韦尔孤儿学校

在一个地方。查理后来说，他的童年就此结束了。那时，他才七岁。

汉韦尔孤儿学校的老师都十分严格，他们用藤条来惩罚孩子。有一次，查理因为没有告发一些做恶作剧的男孩而被藤条抽打。因为他用左手写字，老师会严厉地敲打他的指关节。当查理因为有头癣而被剃光头发时，他崩溃得哭了。

做白日梦是查理最爱的逃避现实的方式。在查理的自传中，他回忆道："我一个人悄悄地溜出了济贫院，假装自己是一个非常富有和出色的人。"

最重要的是，这个小男孩想摆脱贫困。不久后，表演将成为查理走出贫民窟的门票。他很快就找到了第一份工作。

第二章

登台演出

1898 年的秋天，警方联系上查理的父亲，让他收留他的儿子们。你一定会认为查理觉得去哪里都比待在济贫院好。但他说，与和父亲在一起的两个月相比，在济贫院的经历是“一块糖果”。与老查尔斯一起生活的女人并不想跟查理、悉尼住在一起。当他们的父亲不在时，她命令孩子们离开房子。有时兄弟俩不得不依偎在门口，睡在小巷里。

最终汉娜出院了，带走了他们。男孩们再也没有和他们的父亲住在一起过。仅仅过了三年，老查尔斯就死于酗酒，享年三十八岁。

查理开始断断续续地上学，但他经常旷课。1898 年是他在学校的最后一个全日制学年，当时他只有九岁。

当查理旷课时，他便想方设法地挣点钱。一种方法是在街上为一个演奏手风琴的音乐家跳木屐舞。路人会把硬币扔到帽子里。

一天下午，一位衣着考究的绅士观看了他的舞蹈。这位绅士名叫威廉·杰克逊，他管理着一个在伦敦的杂耍剧院里表演木屐舞的少年舞团，这个舞团被称为兰开夏八童子班。现在，杰克逊只有七个小伙子。因为有了查理，他就找到了舞团的第八个男孩。当汉娜同意后，查理开始了他的第一份真正的工作。

查理认为他走了大运！兰开夏八童子班里的四个男孩是杰克逊夫妇的孩子。但这对善良的夫妇把所有的舞者视如己出。查理的食宿都是免费的。他每周挣大约一美元，这笔钱他会寄回家给他的母亲。

舞团的小伙子们都刻苦训练。木屐舞者们会把手臂放在身体两侧，双脚则随着音乐的节拍舞动。

在有演出的晚上，舞者们会乘坐马车从一个杂耍剧院赶往下一个杂耍剧院。查理喜欢看其他的表演，尤其是小丑和喜剧演员的表演。“他们的每一个举动像一张张照片一样刻在我年轻的脑海里，”他说，“我回家后经常自己试着模仿。”查理还学会了变戏法和杂耍表演。

在童子班待了两年多之后，查理的母亲把他带回了家里，她认为她的儿子看起来疲惫不堪。但查理并没有停止工作，他经常打零工。他在理发店、诊所和文具店打过零工。他在印刷厂做过帮工，还给一名玻璃吹制工当过助手。多年后，许多这样的工作场景也出现在了查理的电影中。

尽管如此，钱始终不够用。查理和他的母亲住在顶

楼的一间小房间里（悉尼当时在出海）。汉娜的小铁床就在一个角落里，查理则睡在一张展开的扶手椅充当的床上。

1903 年，查理对母亲的精神状态感到心慌。汉娜似

乎对现实生活失去了把握。汉娜会在几个小时里一动不动地凝视着窗外。脏盘子堆积如山。有时她甚至会听到幻想中的声音。

一天，汉娜挨家挨户地分发包裹好的煤块当作礼物。查理知道他的母亲需要他无法给予的照顾，于是他陪她去了最近的诊所，在一英里[1]外。在那里，医生把汉娜送进了精神病院。在接下来的十七年里，除了短暂的一段时间，她将在不同的医院里度过。

查理独自回到空荡荡的公寓。橱柜里除了一些茶叶

① 英里：英美制长度单位。1 英里≈ 1.609 千米。

之外什么都没有。他在街上徘徊，寻找食物和工作。那时，他听到消息说，他哥哥的船要进港了。“如果悉尼没有回到伦敦，我可能会成为伦敦街头上的小偷。”查理说。

悉尼看到查理破烂的衣衫和又长又脏的头发，大为震惊。悉尼很快带他洗了个热水澡，剪了个头发，买了一套新西装。然后悉尼制订了自己的计划：他要开始演出了。查理也决定试一试。

卓别林兄弟很快就找到了剧院里的工作。查理在《夏洛克·福尔摩斯》中扮演一个小男孩。得到这份工作使他激动不已，这份激动之情持续到了他拿到剧本的时候。由于没怎么上过学，他根本读不懂！

汉娜·卓别林 (1865—1928)

1903年，汉娜·卓别林精神崩溃后就再也没有彻底康复过。即使她的儿子们在加利福尼亚州的海边给她买了一间小屋（1921年），她也不得不在看护的护理下度过余生。她于1928年在那间小屋中去世，享年六十三岁。

查理更乐意回忆他母亲身体好的时候。“在我看来，我的母亲是我认识的最出色的女人，”他告诉记者，“我还记得她是多么迷人，多么有风度。”

于是悉尼大声朗读这些台词给查理听，直到三天后，查理把它们背熟了。在他的余生中，查理依然可以逐字逐句地背诵出这出戏的台词。

《夏洛克·福尔摩斯》一炮而红。这部剧查理出演了两年多。到最后，他决心以表演为生。

他只是不知道他将会以喜剧为生。

第三章

滑稽喜剧

弗雷德·卡诺

1908 年，查理站在弗雷德·卡诺的办公室里面试工作。这位演出经理人是个健壮的家伙，常常抽着一支大雪茄。他管理着一个著名的滑稽喜剧剧团。滑稽喜剧充满拳打脚踢、摔倒、四仰八叉、身体碰撞和扔在脸上的馅饼。

查理的哥哥悉尼已经在为卡诺工作了。但卡诺认为查理根本不适合这份工作。查理的身高只有五英尺[①]四英

① 英尺：英美制长度单位。1 英尺≈0.305 米。

寸（约 162 厘米）[1]。他的手和脚都很小。“我觉得他看起来太害羞了。”卡诺说。

“十七岁是很年轻的年纪，”卡诺告诉查理，“你甚至看起来更年轻。”

查理耸耸肩说这不是什么大问题，只是“化装的问题”。

卡诺同意试用这个少年两周。

在他初次登场的当晚，查理背对着观众上台。他们看到一位富裕的绅士戴着礼帽，披着别致的斗篷。接着查理转过身来。

他把鼻子涂成了鲜红色！

① 英寸：英美制长度单位。1 英寸≈ 2.54 厘米。

观众席传来一阵笑声。于是查理开始扮小丑。他转身穿过舞台时被一个哑铃绊倒了。当他把手杖放在一个直立的拳击袋上时，它打到了他的脸。查理踉踉跄跄地向后仰，并把手杖举到头的一侧。观众哄堂大笑。

到了周末，查理一上台，观众就拍手叫好。卡诺知道他得到了一名会成功的演员。他当即签下了查理。

卡诺的无声喜剧团在英国和欧洲的各大杂耍剧院演出。一周七天，查理每晚都演出三场。

排练占据了所有的时间。在舞台上，演员们表现得看上去很笨拙或是喝醉了，但实际上为了制造笑料，他们需要丝毫不差地掌握时机，就像表演高难度舞蹈一样。这是为什么呢？因为滑稽喜剧往往需要一些连锁反应。第一名演员可能会挥拳，第二名演员则会躲开，而第三个人就会被拳头打中。不过，从来没有人受伤。在台下，有人对每一个假动作都拍手叫好。

查理很快就成了一名擅长表演夸张摔倒的专家。他让最难的杂技表演看起来很容易。很快，卡诺把查理从

小角色培养成了主角。1910 年秋天，他给了查理一个去美国巡演的机会。

卡诺剧团于 9 月下旬抵达纽约市。那天晚上，查理

正沿着百老汇大街散步。剧院的灯光在四周闪烁，摩天大楼在他的头顶若隐若现。查理认为美国提供了机遇和冒险。“这就是我的归属！”他告诉自己。查理当时就下定决心要留下来。

美国人也很喜欢查理。人们对他的表演赞不绝口：卓别林是“最会制造笑声的人”。他是一名“天生的喜剧演员”。光是他的出场就“让整个屋子沸腾了”。

然而，在台下，查理却是一个沉默寡言的人。有些人认为查理是一个不友好的人，他的室友斯坦·劳雷尔对此说：“他不是，他根本不是……他只是一个非常害羞的人。”（劳雷尔后来在劳雷尔和哈迪的喜剧表演中成名。）

斯坦·劳雷尔

在穿行于全国各地的火车长途旅行中，查理总在埋头看书。他的学业被中断得过早，查理决心通过阅读来自学。他还自学了拉小提琴。最开始，查理不得不把琴弦转过来，这是唯一能使他用左手演奏的方法。

1913 年的一天，查理收到了一封电报。那时，他已经在卡诺的剧团里待了五年。这封电报邀请他来加利福尼亚拍电影！

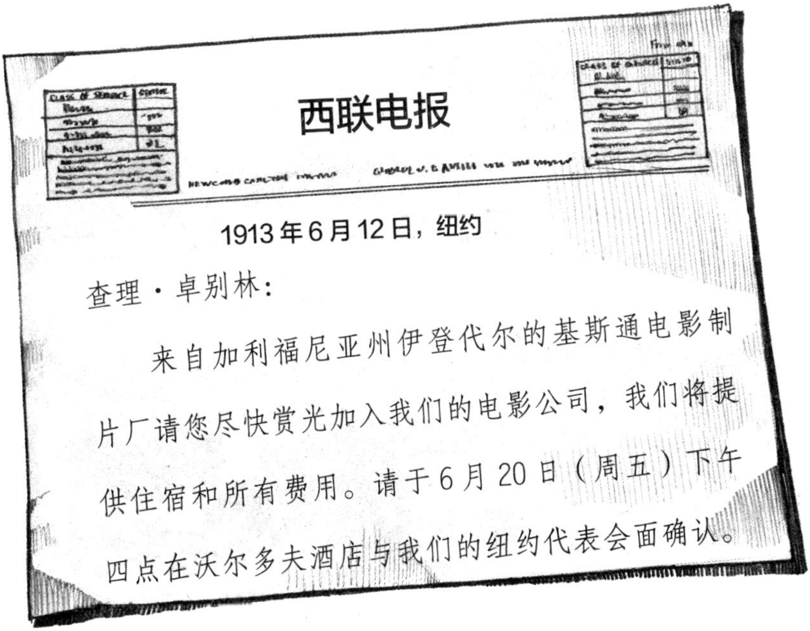

西联电报

1913 年 6 月 12 日，纽约

查理·卓别林：

来自加利福尼亚州伊登代尔的基斯通电影制片厂请您尽快赏光加入我们的电影公司，我们将提供住宿和所有费用。请于 6 月 20 日（周五）下午四点在沃尔多夫酒店与我们的纽约代表会面确认。

这是一次巨大的冒险。查理之前都是在舞台上表演，而不是在镜头前。况且电影业当时还很年轻，八年前，美国第一家电影院刚刚开业。

“我讨厌离开（卡诺剧团），”查理后来说，“假如我做不好呢？”

别担心，查理！

第四章

大银幕

1913 年 12 月，查理在基斯通制片厂里首次亮相了。刚刚成立一年的基斯通制片厂是在阳光明媚的加利福尼亚兴起的几家小型电影制片厂之一。它最受欢迎的电影是关于“基斯通警察”的，讲的是一群笨手笨脚的警察在疯狂的追捕中四处奔波的故事，每部电影中都有同一批演员。

在巡逻车里的“基斯通警察”

摄影棚离洛杉矶有五英里远。对查理来说，它看起来像一个又大又矮的仓库。附近有古老的农场、木屋和商店，还有仙人掌和灌木丛。摄影棚里的演员们看起来像大老粗。查理见状转过身，直接回了旅馆！

三天后，查理还是回到了基斯通制片厂。一个巨大平台（有两个街区那么长）拉长了摄影棚的长度。三四部不同的电影会同时拍摄。布景并排矗立着，其中一个

可能是客厅，另一个是监狱，第三个可能是溜冰场。查理被这些场景迷住了。

摄影棚里一片喧闹。木匠们锯木头、敲钉子来搭建新的布景。摄像机转动着，导演们大声发号施令。当然，喧闹声一点也不重要：电影没有声音。

摄影棚当时也没有使用电灯。尽管当时电灯已经被人们广泛使用，但并没有一种电灯的功率足以曝光胶片。相反，加利福尼亚明亮的阳光照亮了摄影棚。

查理有几天时间来四处看看电影是如何制作的。有些事情让他很惊讶。在一名女演员敲门后，他听到一位导演大喊“停！”。就在那时，查理了解到电影是由小片段组成的。这些场景是无序拍摄，再在剪辑室被拼接到一起的。

当查理准备好扮演他的第一个角色时，又出现一件令他惊讶的事：基斯通制作的电影没有剧本。导演们在开始拍摄时对故事只有一个大概的想法。大部分笑料都是演员和导演在现场编出来的。查理写道：“在剧院里，我被限制在一个又一个晚上的重复、刻板表演中，但电影更自由，它们给了我一种冒险的感觉。”

几天后，查理的第一部电影《谋生之路》（1914）完成了。当时的电影被称为“短片”，片长一卷约十五分钟。基斯通经常一周拍三部电影！

《谋生之路》中的一幕，查理位于左侧

为了拍摄查理的第二部电影，演员们将开车去加利福尼亚州威尼斯市附近的一个儿童德比赛车比赛现场。

麦克·森尼特

基斯通的电影通常在“外景”拍摄，而不是在摄影棚内拍摄。例如，一部电影可能是在游行现场、户外音乐会、赛马现场甚至当地的火灾中拍摄的。现实生活中的场景很有趣，而且这样做制作成本很低。麦克·森尼特是基斯通的负责人，在演员们前往威尼斯之前，他让查理搭配好戏服。查理可以随心所欲地穿衣服。

查理在基斯通的大化妆间——一个旧谷仓——里找了找，找到了他喜欢的东西。他后来写道：“我想要所有的东西都是矛盾的：裤子要宽松的，外套必须紧身，帽子偏小，鞋子却偏大。”

穿好衣服后，查理把一双打了补丁的大鞋子穿反了。然后，他贴上黑色的小胡子，抓起一根手杖，蹒跚地走

到户外。

他当时并不知道，他即将创造历史。

查理刚刚创造了一个著名的角色，后来被人们称为“小流浪汉”。《威尼斯儿童赛车》(1914)是第一部有“小流浪汉”这一角色的电影。两天后，他又出现在《梅布尔的困境》(1914)中，在那部电影中，小流浪汉滑稽的个性生动地体现出来了。他绊倒了一位女士并举起帽子向她道歉。然后，他踉踉跄跄地走过一个痰盂，也向它致意。他优雅地转了转手杖，打掉了自己的帽子。

随着拍摄的进行，查理听到摄影师开始大笑。很快，基斯通剧组的其他人也离开了自己的片场去看他的小丑表演。“这确实是一种赞美，”查理后来回忆道，“我当时就决定，无论发生什么，我都会坚持穿这套服装（坚持演小流浪汉的角色）。”

正如查理所说，他在接下来的二十二年里，在大约七十部电影中扮演了小流浪汉。他只用了短短五天的时间，就塑造了银幕上有史以来最著名的角色之一！

第五章

是导演也是明星

电影让查理着迷了。他开始学习制作电影的每一个环节。影片是如何在剪辑室里剪辑、拼接的？演员可以在哪里移动并仍然留在镜头范围内？摄像机该以怎样的速度来拍摄，从而达到加快或放慢动作的效果？（为了达到喜剧效果，无声电影里人的动作速度往往比现实生活中更快。）

没有人比查理更努力工作了。“他想工作——而且几乎一直都在工作，”麦克·森尼特说，“我们八点去上班，他七点就在那儿了。我们五点下班……但他六点还在。”

不幸的是，查理的风格有时与基斯通的风格相冲突。他们的喜剧聚焦于一场混乱的追逐，查理认为最好的喜剧是以人物性格为基础的，他想在他的戏中加入一些有趣的细节，这些细节体现了小流浪汉的个性，但导演们不想放慢超高速的故事节奏。查理表演的一些最有趣的片段最终只会被“剪掉”。

查理便开始梦想可以自己创作和导演电影。

有一部电影的导演是女演员梅布尔·诺曼德。她当时是个明星。

梅布尔·诺曼德

在一次外景拍摄中，她拒绝听取查理的任何想法。最后查理走了，在马路边坐了下来。

无声电影 1894—1929

电影是用大卷胶片制作的。

摄像机是用手转动的。

电影院里的现场音乐营造了气氛。

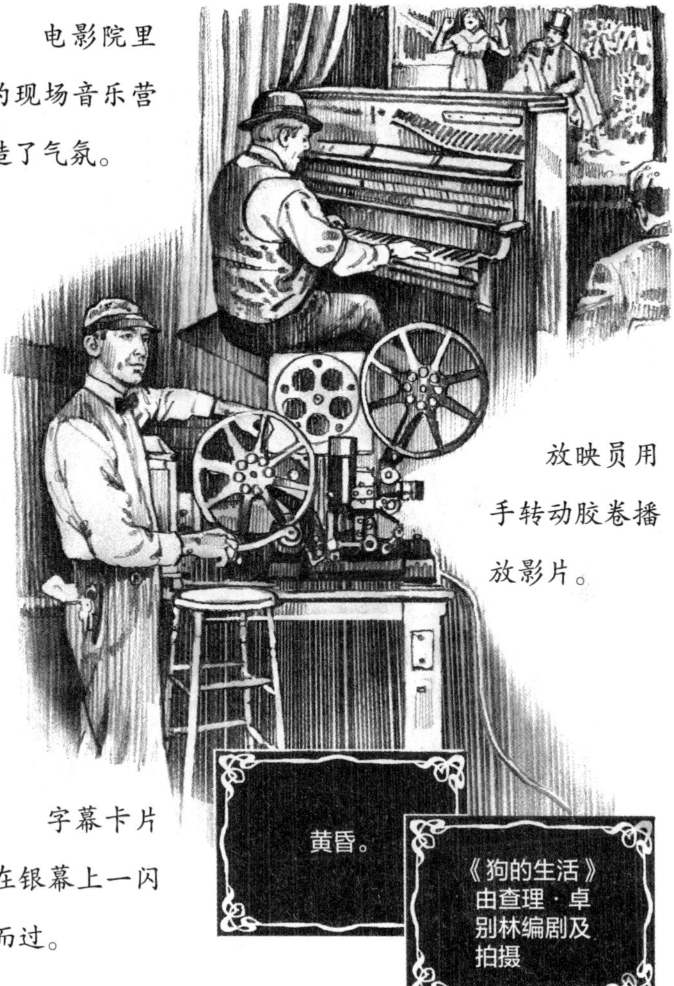

放映员用手转动胶卷播放影片。

字幕卡片在银幕上一闪而过。

麦克·森尼特听到查理静坐罢工的消息后勃然大怒。“照吩咐做！”他对查理喊道，然后他便大步离开了。

查理以为他会被解雇。但令他惊讶的是，第二天森尼特对他还是笑脸相迎。森尼特刚从他在东海岸的老板们那里得知，查理的电影票房超过了基斯通制作的其他所有电影！老板们想马上拥有更多关于那个有趣的“小流浪汉”的电影。

森尼特必须想办法让查理开心。查理提出，他可以自己执导自己出演的电影。森尼特觉得这听起来很冒险。毕竟，查理在拍电影方面还是个新手。随后，查理说他会把自己的毕生积蓄都押上，基斯通不会损失一分钱。这样他们就达成了协议。从那时起，查理既是他自己电影的导演又是其中的明星演员。

查理喜欢为小流浪汉想新的笑料。他总是做出人意料的事。小流浪汉不知道如何挤牛奶，所以会拉扯牛尾巴。当小流浪汉被水管里的水淋得湿透时，他扭了扭耳朵，水却从嘴里流了出来。被自己的影子绊了一下，小流浪汉就向它脱帽致意。

在转换场景的时候，查理会跳木屐舞或倒立来娱乐

剧组人员。为了指导他的演员们，查理会在拍摄前表演一遍所有人的角色。

在那个时候，买一张电影票仅需花费五美分或十美分。电影在许多由旧商店改建而成的名为“五分钱戏院”的小影院里上映。有时查理会溜进正在放映他的电影的电影院里。没有人能认出那个长着一双深蓝色眼睛的英俊青年，他一点也不像电影里那个滑稽的小流浪汉。查理不会看大银幕，他的目光和听力都集中在观众身上。他们什么时候笑的？是什么让他们捧腹大笑？观众的反馈有助于查理塑造他的下一部电影。

五分钱戏院

最早的一批电影院是五分钱戏院，非常受到数百万移民在内的工人阶级的喜欢。

五分钱戏院是破旧而简陋的。那里没有点心供应，观众就坐在木板凳上。观众只需花五美分就可以观看十到十五分钟的黑白短片。

到那时为止，电影演员的名字还没有出现在银幕上。接着，观众想知道留着小胡子的那个人究竟是谁，小流浪汉的大幅海报就开始出现在美国各地的影院前。“查理·卓别林今天在这里。”指示牌上写着。卓别林的名字吸引了很多人。

在基斯通工作了一年后，查理便做好了离开的准备。一年的时间并不长，但是他已经拍了三十五部电影了！

第六章

成名

查理请他的哥哥悉尼做他的业务经理，事实证明这是明智之举。悉尼为查理与艾森奈电影制片厂签订了一份合同，他们付的钱大约是基斯通的三十倍！

查理开始一个月推出一部小流浪汉喜剧。大多数是两胶卷长，片长约为半个小时。但每一场戏都要拍摄好几个小时，查理无休止地重拍。电影《流浪汉》(1915)中的一名演员向斯坦·劳雷尔讲述了他拍摄了五十次爬梯子场景的经历。劳雷尔说：“演员们觉得，如果再重拍一次，他们就会大发雷霆。”但查理是个伟大的艺术家，“他只是想达到最完美的效果。”

在银幕上，查理让一切看起来很轻松。粉丝们开始了解并喜爱他的搞笑风格。小流浪汉在拐角处脚底打

滑时会把一只脚悬空。他会把火柴扔向身后，并用脚后跟踢它一脚。他会把帽子卷到手臂的长度，让它从头上弹下来，而不需要碰到它。小流浪汉还会疯狂地翻跟头——向前翻，向后翻，或翻四分之三个跟头。就在恶作剧开始之前，他会抬起眉毛或抽动他的胡子。

最重要的是，小流浪汉代表了一个永不放弃的小家伙。他的精神在《流浪汉》的著名结局中大放异彩。他刚刚因为一个高大英俊的男人失去了自己的心上人。在一个淡出镜头中，他独自在一条长长的路上蹒跚而行，一条扎在棍子上的手帕搭在他的肩膀上。突然，小流浪汉快乐地单脚蹦了起来，并转动了他的手杖。生活可能会击倒他，但小流浪汉总是会重新振作起来。

1916 年，悉尼把查理叫到纽约，让他与谬区尔电影公司签订新合同。查理坐火车去了那里，到阿尔伯克基那一站时，他听到外面有欢呼声。有消息说查理在那趟火车上，粉丝们便围到站台上去看他。

“卓别林热”席卷美国。商店出售着小流浪汉玩偶、纽扣、漫画书、帽子和扑克牌。美国还举办了小流浪汉模仿大赛。在欧洲，查理很快就成了超级明星，因为无声电影无须翻译。在西班牙，他们称查理为“卡利托斯”，并为他欢呼。在法国，他被称为“夏洛”。在意大利，他被称为“卡洛”。

查理对富裕的向往现在实现了，这是他做梦也想不到的。1916 年，他和谬区尔签的合同规定公司每周付给他一万美元，这使他成为美国乃至全世界收入最高的人。

在一个二十五美分可以买一打鸡蛋的时代，这是一笔可观的收入。仅仅一年后，他就与第一国家影片公司签订了一份合同，这使他成了百万富翁！他实现了白手起家。

悉尼·卓别林

1885 年，悉尼的母亲汉娜嫁给老查尔斯·卓别林时，他还是个婴儿。老查尔斯收养了悉尼，让他姓“卓别林”。四年后，查理出生了。

悉尼最开始当了几年海员，后来成了一名出色的演员。他在卡诺的剧团里晋升成了男主角，在那里他还帮他的弟弟找到了一份工作。后来，查理又帮悉尼在基斯通找到了一份演员的工作，并以此来回报哥哥的恩情。在演戏的同时，悉尼还担任了查理的业务经理，两人赚得盆满钵满。

卓别林兄弟俩一生都很亲密。悉尼很稳重体贴，一直细心地照顾着小查理。悉尼曾给他写道：“自从母亲生病，我们在这个世界上就只有彼此了。”

悉尼在欧洲度过了他的晚年时光，并在那里去世，享年八十岁。

第七章

新电影制片厂

查理一直很节省开销，之前他住在一套只有两个房间的公寓里，但后来他终于开始消费了，他买了他的第一辆车，那是一辆七座的蒸汽自动轿车，他还雇了一个司机，这个司机后来为他工作了二十年。他还雇了一个秘书和一个管家。

他的社交生活仍然平静。热闹的好莱坞派对对他来说一点吸引力都没有。他既不喝酒也不抽烟。不过，在家里，他是个迷人热情的主人。

道格拉斯 · 范朋克

他最好的朋友是道格拉斯 · 范朋克，道格拉斯 · 范朋克是主演《罗宾汉》系列电影的大明星。这两个男人的性格是截然不同的。道格拉斯性格外向，查理则内向。但他们都有冒险精神和生动的幽默感，而且都热爱网球。

查理的大部分时间都花在了工作上。他创作、导演、主演和剪辑了自己所有的电影。他也亲自选角。在《狗的生活》(1917）中，一只名叫斯凯普的流浪狗成了小流浪汉的朋友。查理为拍摄此片让几只纯种狗试了镜，但都没有选用。然后他在当地的流浪狗收容所里找到了一只名叫穆特的小狗。查理感到十分高兴，让它出演了这部电影，并让它留下来当制片厂的吉祥物。

那一年，查理开始建造自己的制片厂。他在好莱坞中心的日落大道买了五英亩[①]地。制片厂里种满了柠檬树和桃树。他建造了一个大花园，还建了一个游泳池和一个网球场。这个梦工厂被设计成一排英国小屋的样子，里面有办公室、舞台、更衣室，还有一个制作胶卷的地方——当然还有一个剪辑室。1918 年，制片厂竣工。卓别林走到制片厂外湿漉漉的水泥地上，留下了自己的脚印。它们是小流浪汉穿着特大号靴子留下的外八字脚印。

---

① 英美制面积单位。1 英亩≈ 4046.86 平方米。

此时，美国正在参加第一次世界大战。查理决定让小流浪汉穿上军装。这个小家伙却不太称职。在电影《从军记》(1918)中，一名严厉的中士命令小流浪汉直线前进，但他的脚一直向外拐。为了准备战斗，小流浪汉带上了应急物资：比如咖啡壶、奶酪刨丝机和打蛋器！

当电影快拍完时，查理担心它不够好笑，他准备把它扔进垃圾桶。然而他的朋友道格拉斯·范朋克看了一些镜头后笑到流泪。查理继续拍摄并发布了这部电影之后，观众也笑哭了。《从军记》一炮而红。当小流浪汉向敌人凯撒的屁股踢出他著名的后踢时，从战争中归来的美国大兵们欢呼起来。

查理仍然在他那只有两个房间的公寓里过着幸福又简朴的生活。《从军记》上映三天后，这个著名的单身汉娶了一名叫米尔德丽德·哈里斯的年轻女演员，这让所有人都感到惊讶。查理随后买了他名下的第一栋房产。不幸的是，查理和米尔德丽德几乎没有共同语言。两年后，这段婚姻便结束了。

查理与米尔德丽德·哈里斯

1919 年，查理与其他好莱坞明星一起成立了一家公司，投资并发行他们自己的电影。这家公司叫联美电影公司，时至今日仍然很有名气。

作为制作人，查理可以随心所欲地拍他想拍的电影。他想拍摄更长、更戏剧化的电影。

第八章

卖座好片

当时，查理正在看一个叫杰基·库根的小男孩在杂耍剧院的舞台上跳一支活泼的舞蹈。这个孩子迷住了观众，就像查理像他那么大时所做的那样。查理想到了一个新点子：拍一部关于孤儿的电影。孩子们已经在电影中出现过了，但是他们几乎从未担任过主角。

杰基·库根

《寻子遇仙记》(1921) 不同于查理的其他电影。这是他所导演的第一部长篇电影，片长一个多小时。这部电影没有将场景松散地组合在一起，而是顺着故事情节演下去。最重要的是，它融合了喜剧和戏剧。片头的字幕上写着：

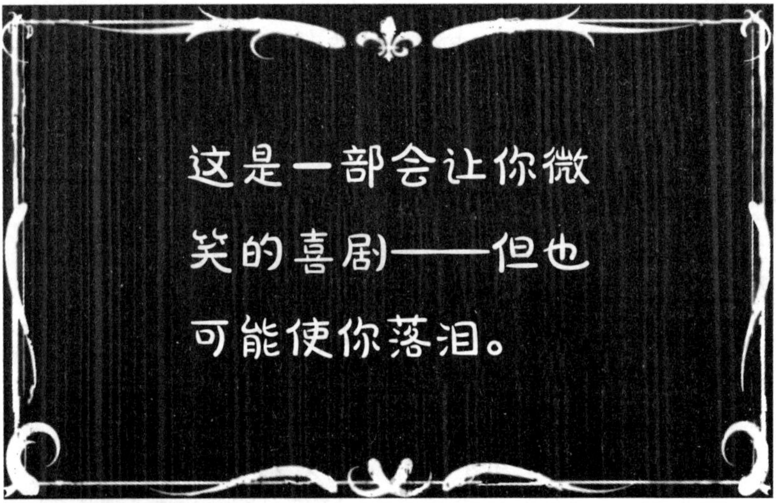

“这行不通，”一位著名编剧警告查理，“(一部电影必须) 要么是滑稽喜剧，要么是戏剧。你不能把它们混合在一起。”但和往常一样，查理听从了自己的直觉。

这部电影讲述了小流浪汉抚养一个无家可归的孩子的故事，这个孩子由杰基·库根扮演。这对乐天的伙伴靠他们的智慧活了下来。

尽管查理有时会对其他演员大发雷霆，但他和他年幼的搭档之间的关系却越来越融洽。在影片的高潮部分，社会工作者们把杰基从小流浪汉的怀里拽走，这是小流浪汉第一次在大银幕上哭泣。他跑过屋顶，跳上卡车去救杰基。看到这里，电影院里没有人能忍住眼泪。

《寻子遇仙记》被誉为杰作。查理把滑稽喜剧提升为艺术，很快这部电影就风靡全球。法国甚至宣布它的首映日为国定假日！

历史给了查理下一部电影的灵感，这次的故事发生在阿拉斯加淘金热期间。19 世纪 90 年代末，成千上万的矿工前往阿拉斯加寻找黄金。在《淘金记》(1925) 中，查理花了一大笔钱打造了看起来像阿拉斯加的布景。他带来十只哈士奇犬和一只活灰熊。成吨的盐和面粉被卡车运来，用来建造一片假雪原。一车车的纸屑被用来制造暴风雪场景。

电影片头在加利福尼亚的内华达山脉拍摄。查理雇了六百名群众演员来扮演掘金人。在一场难忘的戏中，

他们排成纵队，爬上孤零零的山。随后银幕上闪烁出一行字幕：

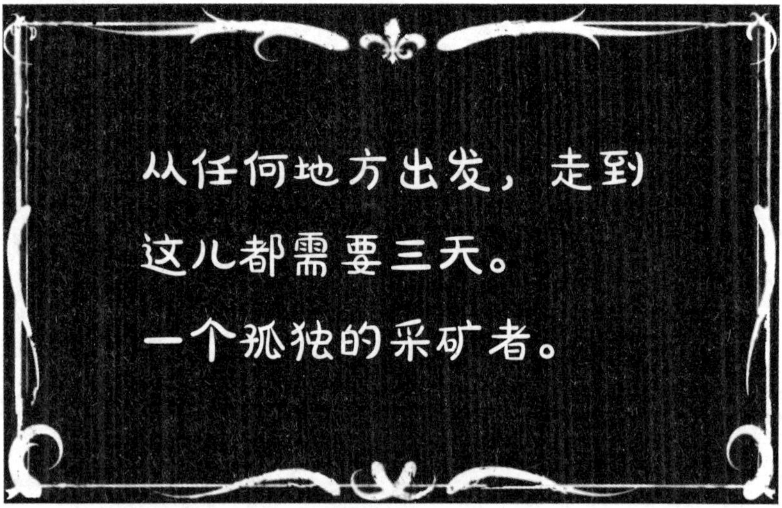

其中有小流浪汉，他拖着脚步沿着冰冷的悬崖前行。当然，他的圆顶礼帽戴在他的头上，手杖也握在他的手里。不久后，饥饿的小流浪汉开始煮他的靴子当感恩节晚餐。他把它当成一种特殊的款待，假装鞋带是意大利面。

后来，流浪汉做了一个举办晚宴的梦。他把叉子戳

进两个晚餐面包卷里，并假装它们是一双正在跳舞的鞋子。观众非常喜欢这一幕，一些影院不得不停下来反复播放它。

影迷和评论家都很喜欢《淘金记》。“卓别林是个天才！”一位评论家在《纽约先驱论坛报》上写道。

虽然查理的电影事业蒸蒸日上，但他的家庭生活却

利塔·格雷

受到了影响。他经历了第二次离婚。尽管他和妻子利塔·格雷育有两个儿子，但他们的婚姻却非常不幸福。查理一直专注于工作，几乎没有时间留给家人。利塔对自己一个人被困在家里的生活感到十分愤怒，她还把这一点告诉了记者。1927 年，卓别林夫妇的离婚事件登上了各大报纸的头条。查理的私生活变得一点也不私密。后来，这些对他性格的攻击再次困扰着他。

离婚期间，查理正在拍摄《马戏团》(1928)。这部电影将成为他连续创作的第三部杰作。片中，小流浪汉背着猴子在高空中走钢索。这暗藏危机的空中走钢索场景反映了查理的真实生活。

第九章
“小流浪汉”谢幕

20世纪20年代末，无声电影的世界发生了翻天覆地的变化。电影可以配上录音来制作了！很快，“有声电影”风靡一时。观众第一次听见了银幕上明星的声音。不幸的是，有些人的口音很重，有些人声音又细又尖。这些人的事业一落千丈。

查理会怎么做？他知道只要他一开口，小流浪汉的魔力就会消失，所以查理决定逆势而上。1928年，他又拍摄了一部无声电影《城市之光》(1931)。观众仍然听不见小流浪汉讲话的声音，但他们听到了他的打嗝声！在一个搞笑的场景中，小流浪汉吞下了哨子，并像小鸟一样啾啾地打了嗝！

在此之前，无声电影的背景音乐是由当地电影院的

钢琴师和风琴手提供的。现在查理可以自己创作音乐了。他便开始创作自己的歌曲！也许他继承了父亲的天赋。查理从来没有学过读乐谱，所以他哼出旋律，再由其他人记下乐谱。查理长长的荣誉称号里又多了一个“作曲家”。

《城市之光》于 1931 年上映。影迷们还会买无声电影的票吗？为了查理，会的！这部电影又成了一部卖座大片。

查理花了三年时间制作《城市之光》。现在是休假的时候了——休一次很长的假期。查理离开好莱坞十六个月，前往欧洲和亚洲。在旅途中，他会见了温斯顿·丘吉尔、圣雄甘地、赫伯特·乔治·威尔斯和萧伯纳等伟人。他还有一次更为私密的停留。

电影院

20 世纪 20 年代，电影院变成了华丽宫殿一般的地方。廉价的五分钱戏院被拥有大理石柱、奢华的木制品和地毯的剧院所取代。有些电影院的建造耗资数百万美元。到 20 世纪 30 年代，剧院开始出售点心。人们开始把爆米花的香味与电影联系起来。

位于洛杉矶的格劳曼中国剧院

底特律福克斯剧院内部

最大的变化发生在“有声电影”问世的时候。属于无声电影时代的钢琴师和风琴手失去了工作，取而代之的是巨大的扬声器和新的音响设备。

在伦敦的一天，他独自溜走，去了汉韦尔。这所古老的砖砌学校看起来和他七岁去那里时一模一样。查理突然走了进去，当餐厅里的四百个男孩认出他来时，他们十分兴奋。查理脱下帽子，帽子像变魔术一样从他头上跳了下来。他双脚朝外，走了著名的“小流浪汉步伐”。男孩们欢呼尖叫。查理也是他们中的一员，他证明了卑微的出身不会成为任何人的阻碍。

那天晚上，在酒店房间里，查理哭了。他童年的记忆涌上心头。他告诉作家托马斯·伯克，这次访问“是他一生中最棒的情感体验”。

当查理旅行归来时，经济大萧条正席卷全国。数以百万计的人失去了工作，或者为了微薄的薪水做着没有前途的工作。查理对他们深表同情，他决定拍摄一部给人启发的喜剧片。他又一次勇敢地拍了无声电影，但这将是他的最后一部。

《摩登时代》(1936)展示了小流浪汉在工厂流水线上工作的情景。小时候，查理在伦敦为一家印刷厂工作。工厂里隐约可见一台巨大的印刷机。看着这台大机器磨来磨去，查理吓了一跳。“我以为它会吞噬我。”他说。在《摩登时代》中，查理用这段记忆来搞笑。怪物机器的齿轮抓住了小流浪汉，并用齿轮咀嚼着他。

这一滑稽的场面也传达了一个严肃的观点：卓别林担心工厂里的工人有时会被当成机器的零件，而不是人。

在电影的最后一幕，小流浪汉和他的爱人失去了一

切。但小流浪汉让她振作起来，并试图让她微笑，然后两人手牵着手走向远方。

就这样，小流浪汉从电影中消失了。

查理的热门歌曲

查理为《摩登时代》写了一首动人的主题曲，几年后，约翰·特纳和杰弗里·帕森斯填写了歌词。这首歌成了一首名为《微笑》的热门歌曲。歌词体现了小流浪汉积极进取的精神：

“微笑吧，尽管心痛。微笑吧，即使心碎。”

许多伟大的歌手都录制了《微笑》，包括纳特·金·科尔、迈克尔·杰克逊和芭芭拉·史翠珊。

第十章

放逐生涯

阿道夫·希特勒

第二次世界大战全面爆发于1939年，当时德国独裁者阿道夫·希特勒开始入侵波兰。希特勒和查理的生日仅隔四天。这两个人甚至看起来有点像。有人说希特勒之所以选择留短胡子，是因为他想像小流浪汉一样受欢迎。然而，希特勒公开表示他讨厌卓别林。他认为卓别林是犹太人，希特勒憎恨所有的犹太人。“我没有这个‘荣幸’。”查理声明。

1939年，查理开始拍摄一部电影来嘲笑这名可怕的暴君。《大独裁者》(1940) 成为他的第一部有声电影。查理扮演了两个角色。其中一个是像希特勒一样的独裁者，阿登诺伊德·亨克尔。他的第二个角色是一个沉默寡言又严肃的犹太理发师。

查理展示了希特勒的真实面貌——一个夸夸其谈、胡言乱语、渴望权力的疯子。在电影著名的一幕中，这名独裁者拿着一个地球仪气球翩翩起舞。他蹦蹦跳跳地跳着欢快的芭蕾舞时，地球仪气球在他面前爆炸了。

《大独裁者》大获成功——当然，在德国除外。希特勒不会让它上映的。《纽约先驱论坛报》上的一位评论家写道，这部电影是“对一个疯狂世界的辛辣、滑稽评论”。查理在欧洲战争开始一周后才开始拍摄这部电影。他后来说，如果他知道即将到来的战争的恐怖，他就不会拍摄这部电影了。

尽管这部电影取得了成功，但20世纪40年代对查理来说是非常艰难的几年。他经历了第一次票房失利。那是一部名叫《凡尔杜先生》(1947)的悬疑谋杀片。但更糟糕的是，有人呼吁将他驱逐出境——驱逐出美国。人们怀疑他是个共产主义者。

第二次世界大战结束后，美国和苏联之间关系十分紧张。它们都是超级大国，也是仅有的有能力投掷核弹的国家。虽然两国之间没有发生实际的战争，但这段时期被人们称为冷战时期。

在美国，关于共产主义者会在国内秘密工作以此获得权力的恐慌蔓延开来。美国政府对所有涉嫌“非美国活动”的人举行了听证会。（这意味着他们是共产主义者。）听证会变成了一场政治迫害。这些人失了业，并且发现自己找不到其他工作。好莱坞电影业的从业者往往是受害者。

但为什么查理·卓别林会成为被攻击的目标呢？首先，许多人认为他的政治观点过于激进。此外，他从未成为美国公民。当被问及原因时，他回答：“我是世界公民。”此时，查理已经经历了三次离婚。每次离婚都被暴露在媒体面前，这也损害了查理的形象。查理坚定地说他不是共产主义者。尽管联邦调查局整理了一份超过两千页的关于卓别林的档案，但他们没有发现任何对他不利的东西。

在这场风波中，查理爱上了乌娜·奥尼尔。她是著名剧作家尤金·奥尼尔的女儿，她是一个聪明美丽的女人，并且她很欣赏查理。他们于 1943 年 6 月结婚。在经历了三次失败的婚姻后，查理终于找到了长久的爱情。最终，他们有了八个孩子。

乌娜·奥尼尔与她的父亲尤金·奥尼尔

1952 年，查理带着乌娜和他们的孩子乘船前往欧洲。他们将前往伦敦参加查理的第三部有声电影《舞台春秋》（1952）的首映式。（大多数美国影院老板禁止这部电影上映。）

在海上待了两天后，查理从美国政府得到消息称，在证明自己是一名忠诚的美国公民之前，他不能再次入境。查理很生气，他的第二祖国背叛了他。他决定永远离开美国。

卓别林夫妇在欧洲漫游了一段时间，住在豪华酒店里。后来，仍是 1952 年，查理和乌娜在瑞士买了一处漂亮的房产。在那里，瑞士的阿尔卑斯山和波光粼粼的莱芒湖的景色一览无遗。查理在那里愉快地度过了他人生最后的二十五年。这家人过着富裕的生活。一大群仆人照料着这座建于 18 世纪的有十九个房间的豪宅。园丁和花匠照料着这片三十五英亩的庄园。

在瑞士，查理一直很忙。他为许多自己的无声电影创作了原创配乐。这使他成为有史以来唯一一位为自己的电影写剧本、表演、导演、选角、制作和作曲的电影制作人。他还拍摄了他的最后两部电影，《纽约之王》（1957）和《香港女伯爵》（1967），但这两部电影都不如他早期的电影受欢迎。

在他的晚年，查理的家庭生活比以前更幸福了。查理七十三岁时，他最小的儿子出生了。他已成年的儿子小查尔斯和他的哥哥悉尼也来探望他。查理喜欢在豪宅的大放映室里和孩子们观赏他的老电影。没有人比查理笑得更厉害了。

第十一章

最后一次演出

在瑞士的山丘上散步时，查理回想起他漫长而充实的一生。1964年，他把这一切写在了纸上：从在济贫院的痛苦时光到“卓别林热”的辉煌时光。这个曾经寡言少语的明星写了五百页。《卓别林自传》被翻译成多种语言，成为世界各地的畅销书。

查理的鬈发完全变白了。他通过游泳和打网球来保持健康。他还会和孩子们在院前的草坪上踢足球。最终，七十多岁的时候，他健康的身体开始垮了。拐杖以前是他著名的道具，现在他要用它来帮忙走路了。

到这时，美国对卓别林的态度已经缓和了。过去对可疑共产主义者的恐惧已经消退了。电影历史学家赞扬了查理在电影行业的开拓性作用。他们意识到，他的喜剧是永恒的。1995年的一项调查询问了一些影评人："谁是电影史上最伟大的演员？"他们把查理·卓别林选为第一名。

1972年，卓别林获得了奥斯卡特别奖。获奖原因是"他使电影成为20世纪的一种艺术形式"。

为了领取他的奥斯卡特别奖，查理飞往美国。这是他二十年来第一次来美国。他的第一站是纽约市，为了影片《寻子遇仙记》的重映。

随后他便来到了好莱坞，当他看到杰基·库根，他在《寻子遇仙记》中的那个年轻小助手时，查理泪流满面，对过去拍摄无声电影的美好时光的回忆涌上了心头。

查理对奥斯卡颁奖典礼上的观众如今会对他有什么反应感到紧张。但他的恐惧很快就消失了。当查理上台时，观众起立鼓掌了十二分钟。“哦，你们真是太棒、太可爱了。”他对观众说，眼泪顺着他的脸滑落。

1975 年，英国女王伊丽莎白二世封这个土生土长的

英国人为爵士。那个流浪街头的小家伙现在是查理·卓别林爵士了。

两年后的圣诞节，卓别林在瑞士的家中去世，身边环绕着他心爱的乌娜和孩子们。这是他非凡人生中的最后一幕，查理享年八十八岁。

2016 年是查理成为明星的一百周年。为了纪念这一年，卓别林博物馆在查理和乌娜的瑞士豪宅中开馆。

对查理的赞美从四面八方传来，但查理本人曾经说过："我只是一名想让人们开怀大笑的小喜剧演员。"

查理·卓别林生平年表

1889 年 — 查尔斯·斯潘塞·卓别林于 4 月 16 日出生在伦敦。
1896 年 — 被送往汉韦尔孤儿学校。
1901 年 — 他的父亲老查尔斯·卓别林死于酗酒，享年三十八岁。
1903 年 — 在《夏洛克·福尔摩斯》中出演角色。
1908 年 — 剧团老板弗雷德·卡诺雇查理表演无声喜剧。
1913 年 — 与基斯通制片厂签约。
1914 年 — 创造了“小流浪汉”角色。
1915 年 — 为艾森奈电影公司发布电影《流浪汉》。
1918 年 —《从军记》成为热门影片。
1921 年 — 他的第一部故事片《寻子遇仙记》上映，好评如潮。
1924 年 —《淘金记》开拍。
1931 年 —《城市之光》全球首映。
1936 年 — 以工厂为拍摄背景的《摩登时代》上映。
1940 年 — 二战讽刺喜剧《大独裁者》上映。
1943 年 — 与乌娜·奥尼尔结婚，他们将有八个孩子。
1952 年 — 他的美国签证被吊销。
— 举家迁往瑞士。
1972 年 — 获得奥斯卡特别奖。
1975 年 — 女王伊丽莎白二世封查理为爵士。
1977 年 — 圣诞节在家中去世，享年八十八岁。

世界大事记

1900 年 — 脱逃艺术家哈里·胡迪尼首次在伦敦杂耍剧院演出。

1911 年 — 几家电影制片厂在加利福尼亚的好莱坞开业。

1913 年 — 亨利·福特为福特汽车的大规模生产安装了第一条移动流水线。

1917 年 — 美国参加第一次世界大战（1914—1918）。

1927 年 —《爵士歌王》开启有声电影新时代。

1929 年 — 首届奥斯卡颁奖典礼在好莱坞举行。

1930 年 — 英国用扶贫制度取代济贫院。

1932 年 — 华特·迪士尼制作了他的第一部彩色电影，是一部名为《花与树》的卡通短片。

1941 年 — 日本轰炸珍珠港后，美国加入第二次世界大战（1939—1945）。

1952 年 — 伊丽莎白公主即位，成为英国女王伊丽莎白二世。

1954 年 — 参议员约瑟夫·麦卡锡举行公开听证会，调查被指控为共产主义者的美国公民。

1961 年 — 迪士尼的《101 忠狗》成为热门电影。

1963 年 — 马丁·路德·金在华盛顿争取就业和自由的游行上发表了著名的《我有一个梦想》演讲。

1974 年 — 理查德·尼克松辞去美国总统职务。

Who Was Charlie Chaplin?

In the early 1900s, movie theaters across America rocked with laughter. It was all because of a funny little guy on the big screen. His pants and shoes were too large. His hat and coat were too small. He walked in an oddball way with both feet turned outward. And when his eyes grew big and he twitched his little mustache, the audience couldn't wait to see what trouble he would get into next. The screen character was called the Little Tramp.

Charlie Chaplin was the actor behind the mustache. He invented the Little Tramp. Charlie also wrote, starred, and directed his own movies. The Little Tramp was always broke and out of work. But Charlie himself was the highest-paid actor in the world—and the most famous. He managed all that without saying a word on-screen.

This was the age of silent films. No sound came from the screen. Inventors hadn't yet found a way to record sound for films. Instead, actors used gestures and facial expressions to act out the story, as in a game of charades. There was none better at this than Charlie Chaplin.

Although his "reel life" was filled with humor, Charlie's real life was not. His poor London childhood had been heartbreaking. His father deserted the family. And his mother couldn't care for her children properly because of mental breakdowns. Yet history remembers Charlie with a smile. He was a pioneer in film who tickled America's funny bone.

Chapter 1

Poverty

America was where Charlie became famous. But England was his first home. Charles Spencer Chaplin was born in London on April 16, 1889. His half brother, Sydney, was four years older.

It's not surprising that Charlie grew up to be an actor: Both of his parents were entertainers. They performed in English music halls—theaters that staged shows featuring many song and dance acts as well as comedy routines. His father was a successful actor and songwriter. His mother was a singer.

Charles Chaplin Sr. was easygoing and charming, but he had a bad drinking problem. No one could rely on him for long. When Charlie was just one, his father packed up his songs and left.

Charlie's mother, Hannah, did the best she could on her own. She was small and delicate, with hair so long she could sit on it. Though she faced life with spirit, jobs came and went, and money was often tight.

Still, the little household was happy for a while. Hannah taught Charlie to dance almost as soon as he could stand. To entertain her sons, Hannah pulled costumes and wigs from her trunk and acted out plays that she knew by heart.

One night, Hannah's singing career came to a sudden end. Her voice cracked in the middle of a song. The crowd hissed and booed Hannah off the stage. The frantic manager pushed little Charlie onstage in her place! Charlie was just five, but he had been watching from backstage for years. He knew all the numbers by heart.

As the small boy began to sing and dance, the crowd grew silent. Soon they were laughing and cheering. Then

Music Halls

Music halls hosted live shows with a dazzling variety of acts. Acrobats flew through the air. Ventriloquists spoke through dummies. Singers and dancers performed. There were high-wire walkers, animal trainers, and plate spinners. Most popular of all were the comedy acts.

In the United States, music halls were known as *vaudeville* (VAUD- vill) theaters. The biggest days for vaudeville were the early 1900s. Once movies became popular, music halls and vaudeville gradually faded into history.

they threw pennies onto the stage. Charlie stopped in the middle of the song to scoot around and pick up the money. The crowd laughed even harder.

Charlie was a hit. However, Hannah's career was over. She never sang again. "That night was my first appearance on the stage," Charlie later wrote, "and Mother's last."

The family began sinking deeper and deeper into poverty. Hannah earned a little money sewing, but not enough to pay the bills. She tore up her old costumes to make clothes for her sons. Often short of rent money, the Chaplins were forced to move again and again. They started out in a three-room apartment. Then they moved into two rooms. Finally, they crowded into one room behind a smelly pickle factory.

In time Hannah was too weak and ill to go on. She led her sons to the workhouse. That was where poor people ended up in London when there was no place else to go.

The little family was split apart. Hannah was put in an

infirmary, a place for people too sick to earn their keep in the workhouse. Charlie and Sydney were taken to a school for homeless children, called Hanwell. Charlie clung tightly to his older brother, but Sydney had to stay in a ward with older boys. Charlie later said that his childhood ended right then. He was seven.

Teachers at Hanwell were strict. They used a cane to punish children. One time Charlie was caned for not telling on some boys who had pulled a prank. His knuckles were rapped because he wrote left-handed. When his head was shaved because of ringworm, Charlie broke down and wept.

Daydreaming was Charlie' s great escape. In his autobiography, Charlie recalled "creeping off by myself at the poorhouse and pretending I was a very rich and grand person."

More than anything, the little boy wanted to escape poverty. In time, acting would become Charlie's ticket out of the slums. And he was soon to get his first job.

The English Workhouse

During Charlie's childhood, poor people who couldn't pay their bills were sent to the workhouse. There they worked for their rooms and meals, if they were able. Families were split up and only met briefly, once a day. Everyone wore uniforms, slept in long dorms, and ate on benches in large dining halls. No one wanted to end up in the workhouse. Yet it probably saved many from starving on the streets.

Chapter 2

Onstage

In the fall of 1898, the law caught up with Charlie's father and made him take in his sons. You would think Charlie would prefer anything to the workhouse. But he said that was "a stick of candy" compared to two months with his father. Charles Sr. lived with a woman who didn't want Charlie and Sydney around. When their father was away, she ordered the boys out of the house. Sometimes the brothers had to huddle in doorways and sleep in alleys.

At last Hannah got out of the hospital and rescued them. The boys never again lived with their father. Just three years later, Charles Sr. would die from alcohol abuse at age thirty-eight.

Charlie now attended school off and on— mostly off. 1898 became his last full-time year at school. He was only nine.

When he played hooky, Charlie tried to earn a few pennies. One way was clog dancing on the street for a musician with a barrel organ. Passersby tossed coins into a hat.

One afternoon, a well-dressed gentleman watched his dancing. The man, William Jackson, managed a group of boys who clog danced in music halls around London. They were called the Eight Lancashire Lads. Right now, Jackson had only seven lads. In Charlie, he found his eighth. When Hannah gave her permission, Charlie began his first real job.

Charlie thought he' d hit the jackpot! Four of the Lancashire Lads were children of Mr. and Mrs. Jackson. But the kindly couple treated all the dancers as family. Charlie had a free room. Food was free, too. And he earned about a dollar a week, which he sent home to his mother.

The Lads trained hard. Cloggers hold their arms still at their sides while their feet fly to the beat of the music.

On show nights, the dancers sped from one music hall to the next in horse-drawn carts. Charlie loved to watch the other acts, especially the clowns and comedians. "Every move they made registered on my young brain like a photograph," he said. "I used to try it all when I got home." Charlie also learned to juggle and do acrobatic stunts.

After more than two years with the Lads, Charlie's mother brought him home. She thought her son looked worn out. But Charlie didn't stop working. He often took odd jobs. He worked at a barbershop, a doctor's office, and a stationery store. He became a printer's helper and a glassblower's assistant. Years later, many of these work settings appeared in Charlie's movies.

Still, there was never enough money. Charlie and his mother lived in a tiny top-floor room. (Sydney was away at sea.) Hannah's small iron bed stood in one corner. Charlie slept in an armchair that unfolded into a bed.

In 1903, Charlie grew alarmed at his mother's state of mind. Hannah seemed to be losing her grip on reality. For hours Hannah gazed out the window without stirring. Dirty dishes piled up. Sometimes she heard imaginary voices.

One day, Hannah went door-to-door handing out pieces of wrapped coal as gifts. Charlie knew his mother needed the kind of care he was not able to give. So he walked her to the nearest clinic, a mile away. From there, doctors sent Hannah to a mental hospital. Except for short periods, she would remain in different hospitals for the next seventeen years.

Charlie walked home alone to the empty apartment. The cupboards were bare except for tea. He prowled the streets, looking for food and work. Then word came that his big brother's ship was coming in. "If Sydney had not returned to London, I might have become a thief in the London streets," Charlie said.

Sydney was shocked to see Charlie's rags and long,

Hannah Chaplin (1865–1928)

Hannah Chaplin never fully recovered her mental health after her breakdown in 1903. She had to remain under nursing care for the rest of her life, even after her sons got her a cottage by the sea in California in 1921. She died there in 1928 at age sixty-three.

Charlie always preferred to remember his mother in better times. "It seems to me that my mother was the most splendid woman I ever knew," he told a reporter. "I can remember how charming and well-mannered she was."

dirty hair. He quickly got him a hot bath, a haircut, and a new suit. Then he laid out his plan: Sydney was going to start acting. Charlie decided to try it, too.

The Chaplin brothers soon landed theater jobs. Charlie played a young boy in *Sherlock Holmes*. Getting the job thrilled him—until he got the script. With so little schooling, he couldn't read it! So Sydney read aloud the lines until, in three days, Charlie knew them by heart.For the rest of his life, Charlie could recite the play, word for word.

Sherlock Holmes became a smash hit. Charlie was in the play for over two years. By the end, he was determined to make acting his life.

He just didn't know it would be in comedy.

Chapter 3

Slapstick Comedy

In 1908, Charlie stood in the office of Fred Karno, asking for a job. The showman was a beefy guy who smoked a big cigar. He managed a famous group of slapstick comedians. Slapstick comedy abounds with punches, falls, sprawls, bumps, and pies in the face.

Charlie's brother, Sydney, already worked for Karno. But Karno didn't think Charlie would fit in at all. Charlie stood only five feet four inches tall. His hands and feet were small. "I thought he looked much too shy," said Karno.

"Seventeen's very young," Karno told Charlie, "and you look even younger."

Charlie shrugged and said that wasn't a big problem,

just "a question of make-up."

Karno agreed to try out the teenager for two weeks.

For his opening night, Charlie entered the stage with his back to the audience. They saw a well-to-do gentleman wearing a top hat and fancy cape. Then Charlie turned around.

He had painted his nose bright red!

There was a ripple of laughter. So Charlie started to clown. He veered across the stage, tripping over a dumbbell. When he caught his cane on an upright punching bag, it slapped him in the face. Charlie staggered and swung back, landing his cane on the side of his head. The audience roared.

By the end of the week, the crowd clapped as soon as Charlie came onstage. Karno knew he had a winner. He signed Charlie on the spot.

Karno' s Speechless Comedians performed in music halls all over England and Europe. Charlie performed in three shows a night, seven days a week.

Rehearsals filled the days. Onstage, the players acted clumsy or drunk, but their gags actually required split-second timing, like the steps of a difficult dance. Why? Because slapstick often involves chain reactions. One player might throw a punch, the second guy ducks, and a third man takes the blow. No one ever got hurt, though. Offstage someone clapped sharply at each fake punch.

Charlie quickly became an expert at taking wild tumbles. He made the hardest stunts look easy. Soon Karno raised Charlie from bit parts to starring roles. In the fall of 1910, he offered Charlie a chance to go to America on a tour.

The Karno troupe landed in New York City in late September. That night, Charlie walked along Broadway. Theater lights twinkled all around. Skyscrapers loomed above his head. Charlie thought America offered opportunity and adventure. *This is where I belong!* he told himself. Charlie made up his mind right then and there to stay.

America loved Charlie right back. Rave reviews poured

in for his act: Chaplin is the “biggest laugh-maker.” He is a “born comedian.” His entrance alone “sets the house in a roar.”

Offstage, however, Charlie was quiet and reserved. Some of the guys thought Charlie was unfriendly, said his roommate Stan Laurel. (Laurel later became famous in the Laurel and Hardy comedy act.) “He wasn’t, he wasn’t at all.... He is a very, very shy man.”

During the long cross-country train rides, Charlie buried his nose in a book. His schooling had been cut so short. Now Charlie was determined to educate himself by reading. He also taught himself to play the violin. First Charlie had to reverse the strings. It was the only way he could play left-handed.

One day in 1913, a telegram came for him. By then, Charlie had spent five years with Karno. The telegram invited him to come to California and make movies!

It was a big risk. Charlie had always acted onstage, not

in front of a camera. And the movie business was still young. The first US movie theater had opened its doors just eight years earlier.

"I hated to leave [Karno]," Charlie said later. "Suppose I didn't make good?"

No worries there, Charlie!

Chapter 4

The Big Screen

In December, 1913, Charlie showed up for his first day at Keystone Studios. Only a year old, Keystone was one of several small movie studios that had sprouted up in sunny California. Its most popular movies were about the Keystone Kops, a fumbling group of policemen who dashed around on wild chases. The same group of actors performed in every film.

The studio was five miles outside of Los Angeles. To Charlie, it looked like a big dumpy warehouse. Old farms, wooden shacks, and stores were nearby, along with cactus and sagebrush. The actors at the studio looked like roughnecks. Charlie turned around and went straight back to his hotel!

It took three days before Charlie finally returned to Keystone. A huge platform, two blocks long, stretched the length of the studio. Three or four different movies were filmed at the same time. The sets stood side by side. One might be a living room, another a prison, and a third a skating rink. Charlie was fascinated.

A roar filled the studio. Carpenters sawed lumber and pounded nails to build new sets. Cameras cranked. Directors shouted orders. The racket didn't matter at all, of course: Movies had no sound.

Movie studios didn't use electric lighting at the time, either. Even though electric lights were widely used by then, none were powerful enough to expose film. Instead, bright California sunshine lit the studio.

Charlie was given a few days to look around to see how movies were made. Some things surprised him. He heard a director shout "cut!" after an actress had only pounded on a door. That was when Charlie learned that movies were made in little pieces. The scenes were filmed out of order and later spliced together in the editing room.

When Charlie was ready to play his first role, there was another surprise: Keystone made movies without a script. Directors started filming with only a loose idea of the story. The actors and directors made up most of the gags on the spot. "In the theater I had been confined to a rigid routine of repeating the same thing night after night," wrote Charlie, "but films were freer. They gave me a sense of adventure."

A couple of days later, Charlie's first movie, *Making a Living* (1914), was done. Movies at that time were called "shorts." They were one reel long, or about fifteen minutes. Keystone often made three movies a week!

For Charlie's second movie, the cast was going to drive to a kids' derby-car race in nearby Venice, California. Keystone movies were often filmed "on location" rather than inside a studio. For instance, a movie might be shot at a parade, outdoor concert, horse race, or even a local fire. Real-life scenes were interesting, plus they cost nothing to produce. Mack Sennett was the head of Keystone. Before the cast left for Venice, he told Charlie to put together a costume. He could dress any way he wanted.

Charlie searched through Keystone's large costume room—an old barn—and took whatever caught his fancy. He later wrote, "I wanted everything a contradiction: the pants baggy, the coat tight, the hat small and the shoes large." Once dressed, Charlie pulled a huge pair of patched shoes on the wrong feet. Then he pasted on a small black mustache, grabbed a cane, and shambled outdoors.

He didn't know it then, but he was about to make movie history.

Charlie had just invented the famous character that became known as the Little Tramp. *Kid Auto Races at Venice* (1914) was the first movie with the Tramp in it. Two days later, he appeared in *Mabel's Strange Predicament* (1914), and in that movie the Tramp's funny personality came to life. He stumbles over a lady's foot and raises his hat to apologize. Then he staggers over a spittoon and tips his hat to that, too. He gives an elegant twirl to his cane and knocks off his own hat.

As the filming went on, Charlie heard the cameraman start to laugh. Soon others in the Keystone crew left their sets to watch the clowning. "That indeed was a compliment," Charlie recalled later. "I then and there decided I would keep to this costume [and Tramp character], whatever happened."

True to his word, Charlie played the Tramp for the next twenty-two years in about seventy films. He had created one of the most famous characters ever to appear on-screen after just five days in the movies!

Chapter 5

Director and Star

The movies had Charlie hooked. He set about learning every part of filmmaking. How was film cut and spliced in the editing room? Where could actors move and still stay within the camera range? At what speeds were the cameras cranked to hurry up or slow down the action? (Silent movies often raced at a pace faster than real life, for comic effect.)

No one worked harder than Charlie. "He wanted to work—and nearly all the time," said Mack Sennett. "We went to work at eight o'clock and he was there at seven. We quit at five . . . but he'd still be around at six."

Unfortunately, Charlie's style sometimes clashed with Keystone's. Their comedies focused on a pell-mell chase.

Charlie thought that the best comedy was based on character. He wanted to add funny details to his scenes that played on the Tramp's personality. But directors didn't want to slow down the superfast pace. Some of Charlie's funniest bits ended up on the cutting-room floor. Charlie began to dream of writing and directing his own movies.

For one picture, actress Mabel Normand was the director. She was a star at the time. During an outdoor shoot, she refused to listen to any of Charlie's ideas. Finally Charlie walked off and sat down on the curb.

Mack Sennett was furious when he heard about Charlie's sit-down strike. "Do what you're told," he yelled at Charlie. Then he marched off.

Charlie figured he'd be fired. But to his surprise, Sennett met him with a friendly smile the next day. He had just learned from his bosses on the East Coast that Charlie's films were outselling all other Keystone movies! They wanted more pictures with that funny Tramp guy right away.

Silent Films 1894–1929

Movies were made on big reels of film.

Cameras were cranked by hand.

Live music at the theater set a mood.

Projectionists cranked the film.

Title cards flashed on the screen.

Sennett had to find a way to make Charlie happy. Charlie suggested that he direct his own movies. That sounded risky to Sennett. Charlie was still new to movies, after all. Then Charlie said he'd put his life savings on the line. Keystone would not lose a cent. That sealed the deal. From then on, Charlie was both director and star of his films.

Charlie loved thinking up gags for the Tramp. He always did the unexpected. Not knowing how to milk a cow, the Tramp might pull its tail. When drenched with a hose, the Tramp twisted his ear and water poured from his mouth. Tripping over his shadow, the Tramp tipped his hat to it.

In between scenes, Charlie entertained the crew by clog dancing or doing headstands. To direct his cast, Charlie acted out all their parts before shooting.

A seat at the movies cost only a nickel or dime at that time. Movies were shown in small theaters called nickelodeons, converted from old stores. Sometimes Charlie slipped into a theater where his film was playing. No one recognized the handsome young man with the deep blue eyes. He looked nothing at all like the funny hobo on film. Charlie didn't watch the screen. His eyes and ears were focused on the audience. When did they chuckle? What made them laugh hard? The audience feedback helped Charlie shape his next film.

Up until then, movie actors had not been named on the screen. Now the public demanded to know who *was* that guy behind the mustache? Big cut-outs of the Tramp started popping up in front of theaters all around America. "Charlie Chaplin. I am here today," the signpost read. The Chaplin name became a big draw.

After one year at Keystone, Charlie was ready to move on. A year isn't a very long time. But he had already made thirty-five movies!

Nickelodeons

The first movie theaters were nickelodeons. Working-class people, including millions of immigrants, flocked to them.

Nickelodeons were shabby and poor. No refreshments were served, and viewers sat in wooden chairs. For just a nickel, viewers watched black-and-white shorts lasting ten to fifteen minutes.

Chapter 6

Fame

Charlie asked his brother, Sydney, to be his business manager. It proved to be a wise move. Sydney landed Charlie a contract with Essanay Film Studios. They paid about thirty times as much as Keystone had!

Charlie started to turn out about one Tramp comedy a month. Most were two reels long, lasting about a half hour. But hours and hours of filming went into every scene. Charlie did endless retakes. An actor for *The Tramp* (1915) told Stan Laurel about shooting a ladder scene fifty times. "The actors felt that if they did it one more time they'd blow their corks," Laurel reported. But Charlie was a great artist. "He just absolutely refused to do anything but the best."

On the screen, Charlie made everything look easy. Fans came to know and adore his funny style. The Tramp skidded around corners with one foot in the air. He threw a match over his shoulder and kicked it with his heel. He rolled his hat down the length of his arm and made it spring off his head without touching it. The Tramp did crazy somersaults—forward, backward, and three quarters. Just before mischief started, he arched his eyebrows or twitched his mustache.

Most important, the Tramp stood for the little guy who never gives up. His spirit shines through in the famous ending of *The Tramp*. He has just lost his sweetheart to a tall, handsome man. In a fadeout shot, he trudges along down a long road alone. A bandana on a stick is slung over his shoulder. Suddenly, the Tramp does a happy little hop and twirls his cane. Life might knock him down, but the Tramp always picks himself up again.

In 1916, Sydney called Charlie to New York to sign a new contract with the Mutual Film Corporation. Charlie took the train there. At a stop in Albuquerque, he heard cheers outside. Word had leaked that Charlie was on the train. Fans had mobbed the station to see him.

A Chaplin craze was sweeping America. Stores sold Tramp dolls, buttons, comic books, hats, and playing cards. Tramp look-alike contests were held. In Europe, Charlie became a superstar very quickly because silent movies didn't have to be translated into another language. In Spain, they cheered for *Carlitos*; in France, *Charlot*; in Italy, *Carlo*.

Charlie's longing for wealth now came true beyond his wildest dreams. His Mutual contract of 1916 paid him $10,000 a week. That made him the highest-paid person in America—maybe even the world. It was an outstanding amount in an age when a quarter could buy a dozen eggs. Just a year later, he signed a contract with First National that made him a millionaire! He'd gone from rags to riches.

Sydney Chaplin

Sydney was an infant when his mother, Hannah, married Charles Chaplin Sr. in 1885. Charles adopted Sydney and gave him his last name, Chaplin. Four years later, Charlie was born.

Sydney himself became a fine actor, after first spending several years as a seaman. He rose to leading actor for Karno, where he helped his little brother get a job. Charlie later returned the favor when he helped Sydney get hired as a Keystone actor. While continuing to act, Sydney also served as Charlie's business manager, pulling in superb money deals.

The brothers were very close all their lives. Sydney, stable and caring, kept careful watch over the younger Charlie. Sydney once wrote him, "Since Mother's illness, all we have in the world is each other."

Sydney spent his last years in Europe, where he died at age eighty.

Chapter 7

A New Studio

Charlie had always been careful about money, living in just a two-room apartment. But now he finally started to spend. He bought his first car, a seven-seat Locomobile, and hired a driver who stayed with him for twenty years. He also hired a secretary and butler.

His social life was still quiet. Splashy Hollywood parties didn't appeal to him at all. He neither drank nor smoked. At home, he was a charming host, though.

His best friend was Douglas Fairbanks, the dashing star of the *Robin Hood* movies. The two men were opposites. Douglas was outgoing; Charlie was private. But they shared a sense of adventure, a love of tennis, and a lively sense of humor.

Most of Charlie's time was spent working. He wrote, directed, starred in, and edited all his films. He also did his own casting. In *A Dog's Life* (1917), a stray dog named Scraps becomes the Tramp's pal. Charlie tested— and rejected—several purebred dogs for the part. Then he found a runt named Mutt at the local pound. Delighted, Charlie cast him in the movie and kept him on as a studio mascot.

That year, Charlie began building his own studio. He bought five acres on Sunset Boulevard in the heart of Hollywood. Lemon and peach trees bloomed in the lot. He planted a large garden and put in a swimming pool and tennis court. The dream studio was designed to look like a row of English cottages. Inside were offices, stages, dressing rooms, a place to create the reels—and, of course, a cutting room. In 1918, the studio was finished. Chaplin stepped outside into the wet cement and laid his footprints. They were the Tramp's big boots facing outward.

By this time, the United States was fighting in World War I. Charlie decided to put the Tramp in uniform. The little guy wasn't exactly fit for duty. In *Shoulder Arms* (1918), a stern sergeant orders the Tramp to march in a straight line. But his feet keep springing outward. To prepare for battle, the Tramp takes along emergency supplies: things like a coffeepot, a cheese grater, and an eggbeater!

When the movie was almost done, Charlie feared it wasn't funny enough. He was ready to throw it in the trash can. Then his buddy Douglas Fairbanks saw the footage and laughed till he cried. So did the audience when Charlie went ahead and released the film. *Shoulder Arms* became an instant smash hit. GIs returning from the war cheered when the Tramp delivered his famous back kick to the enemy Kaiser's rear.

Charlie still lived happily and simply in two rooms. Then three days after *Shoulder Arms* opened, the famous bachelor surprised everyone by marrying a young actress named Mildred Harris. Charlie bought the first house he ever owned. Unfortunately, Charlie and Mildred had very little in common. Two years later, the marriage ended.

In 1919, Charlie joined other Hollywood stars to form a company to fund and distribute their own films. Called United Artists, it remains successful to this day.

As a producer, Charlie could do whatever he pleased. What he wanted was to make longer, more dramatic films.

Chapter 8

Blockbusters

Charlie was watching a little boy named Jackie Coogan do a lively dance on a vaudeville stage. The child charmed the audience, just as Charlie had done at that age. A new idea dawned on Charlie: to make a movie about an orphan child. Children had appeared in movies before. But they'd hardly ever held starring roles.

The Kid (1921) was different from Charlie's other films. It was his first full-length movie as a director, lasting an hour. Instead of scenes loosely held together, it followed a storyline. Most important, it mixed comedy and drama. The opening title card read:

A picture with a smile—and perhaps, a tear.

"It won't work," a famous scriptwriter warned Charlie. "[A movie must be] either slapstick or drama. You cannot mix them." But as usual, Charlie followed his instincts.

The movie shows the Tramp raising a homeless child played by Jackie Coogan. The happy-go-lucky pair survives through their wits.

Although Charlie's temper sometimes flared with other actors, an easy bond grew between him and his young co-star. In the film's climax, social workers tear Jackie out of the Tramp's arms. For the first time on screen, the Tramp cries. He races across rooftops and leaps onto a truck to rescue Jackie. By then, there wasn't a dry eye in the house.

The Kid was hailed as a masterpiece. Charlie had raised slapstick to art. Soon the film became a worldwide hit. France declared its opening day a national holiday!

History inspired Charlie's next film, set during the

Alaskan Gold Rush. In the late 1890s, thousands of prospectors went to Alaska in search of gold. In *The Gold Rush* (1925), Charlie spent a fortune to create sets that looked like Alaska. He brought in ten husky dogs and a live grizzly bear. Tons of salt and flour were trucked in to build a fake snowfield. Cartloads of confetti were brought in for the blizzard scenes.

The opening was shot in the Sierra Nevada Mountains of California. Charlie hired six hundred extras to play gold diggers. In an unforgettable scene, they snake up the lonely mountain in single file. Then a card flashes on screen:

> *Three days from anywhere.*
>
> *A Lone Prospector.*

And there's the Tramp, shuffling along an icy cliff. Of course, his bowler hat is on his head and his cane is in his hand. Before long, the starving Tramp is boiling his boot for Thanksgiving dinner. He serves it up like a special treat, pretending the shoelaces are spaghetti.

Later the Tramp has a dream of hosting a dinner party. He jabs forks into two dinner rolls and pretends they're a pair of shoes dancing. Audiences liked the scene so much that some theaters had to stop the movie and replay it.

Fans and critics alike loved *The Gold Rush.* "Chaplin is a genius!" a reviewer wrote in the *New York Herald Tribune.*

While Charlie's film life thrived, his home life suffered. He was going through a second divorce. Though he and his wife, Lita Grey, had two sons together, their marriage was deeply unhappy. Charlie stayed so focused on his work that he left little time for his family. Lita was furious over being stuck at home alone—and she let reporters know it. The Chaplins' divorce in 1927 was splashed all over the headlines. Charlie's private life wasn't private at all. Later, the attacks on his character would come back to haunt him.

During the divorce, Charlie was filming *The Circus* (1928). It would become his third masterpiece in a row. The

Tramp walks a high wire with monkeys on his back. The treacherous tightrope walk mirrored Charlie’s real life.

Chapter 9

The Tramp Exits

In the late 1920s, the world of silent movies was turned upside down. Films could now be made with recorded sound! Soon "talkies" became all the rage. Audiences heard the voices of screen stars for the first time. Unfortunately, some had strong accents or thin, squeaky voices. Their careers went bust.

What would Charlie do? He knew the magic of the Little Tramp would be lost as soon as he uttered a word. So Charlie decided to buck the trend. In 1928, he forged ahead on another silent film, *City Lights* (1931). The audience still doesn't hear the Tramp talk. But they hear his hiccups! In a hilarious scene, the Tramp swallows a whistle and hiccups in tweets!

Before now, background music for silent films had been supplied by piano players and organists in local movie houses. Now Charlie could create the music himself. He started writing his own songs! Perhaps he'd inherited the talent from his father. Charlie had never learned to read music, so he hummed the melody and someone else wrote the notes. "Music composer" was added to Charlie's long list of credits.

City Lights opened in 1931. Would moviegoers still buy tickets for a silent picture? For Charlie, yes! The film became another blockbuster.

It had taken Charlie three years to make *City Lights*. Now it was time for a break—a good long one. Charlie left Hollywood for sixteen months and sailed for Europe and Asia. During the trip, he met with great men like Winston Churchill, Mahatma Gandhi, H. G. Wells, and George Bernard Shaw. He also made a much more private stop.

Movie Theaters

Movie theaters became fancy palaces in the 1920s. The cheap nickelodeons gave way to theaters with marble columns, lavish woodwork, and carpets. Some cost millions to build. By the 1930s, theaters sold refreshments. The smell of popcorn became tied to the movies.

The biggest changes came when " talkies" arrived. The piano players and organists of the silent-movie era lost their jobs. Huge speakers and new sound equipment were installed in place of them.

One day in London, he slipped away by himself and went to Hanwell. The old brick school looked the same as when he'd gone there at seven years old. Charlie stepped inside for a surprise visit. Four hundred boys in the dining room went wild when they recognized him. Charlie went to tip his hat and it sprang off his head like magic. He turned out his feet and did his famous Tramp walk. The boys cheered and screamed. Charlie was one of their own. He proved that humble roots didn't have to hold anyone back.

That night in his hotel room, Charlie wept. Memories of his childhood flooded back. He told the writer Thomas Burke that the visit "had been the greatest emotional experience of his life."

When Charlie returned from his trip, the Great Depression was gripping the country. Millions lost their employment or worked at dead-end jobs for low wages. Charlie felt a deep sympathy for them. He decided to make a comedy with a message. Once again, he dared to do a silent movie. But it would be his last.

Modern Times (1936) shows the Tramp working on a factory assembly line. As a young lad in London, Charlie had worked for a printer. An enormous printing press loomed inside the plant. It scared Charlie to watch the big machine grind and roll. "I thought it was going to devour me," he said. In *Modern Times*, Charlie plays this memory for laughs. The cogs of a monster machine capture the Tramp and the gears chew him. The hilarious scene also had a serious message. Chaplin worried that factory workers were sometimes treated like parts of a machine, not people.

In the final scene of the movie, the Tramp and his sweetheart have lost everything. But the Tramp cheers her up and tries to get her to smile. Then the pair walks into the distance, hand in hand.

With that, the Little Tramp disappeared from film.

Charlie's Hit Song

Charlie composed a deeply moving melody for the theme song of *Modern Times*. Years later, lyrics were added by John Turner and Geoffrey Parsons. It became a hit song called "Smile." The words capture the Little Tramp's positive, winning spirit:

"Smile though your heart is aching.

Smile even though it's breaking."

Many great singers have recorded "Smile," including Nat King Cole, Michael Jackson, and Barbra Streisand.

Chapter 10

Exile

World War II broke out in 1939 when the German dictator Adolf Hitler began his invasion of Poland. Hitler and Charlie had been born just four days apart. The two men even looked somewhat alike. Some say Hitler chose his stubby mustache because he wanted to be popular, like the Little Tramp. Hitler, however, made it known that he hated Chaplin. He thought Chaplin was Jewish, and Hitler hated all Jews. "I don't have the honor," Charlie stated.

In 1939, Charlie started a film to ridicule the awful tyrant. *The Great Dictator* (1940) became his first talking picture. Charlie played two parts. One was Adenoid Hynkel, a dictator like Hitler. His second role was that of a quiet and dignified Jewish barber.

Charlie showed what Hitler was really like—a ranting, raving, power-hungry maniac. In one famous scene, the dictator dances with a balloon globe. He leaps and romps in a joyful ballet. The globe blows up in his face.

The Great Dictator was a great success—except in Germany, of course. Hitler wouldn't let it be shown. A critic for the *New York Herald Tribune* wrote that the movie was "a savage comic commentary on a world gone mad." Charlie had started the film just one week after the war in Europe began. He said later that he would not have made it if he'd known the horrors of the war that were to come.

Despite the film's success, the 1940s were very hard years for Charlie. He had his first box-office flop. It was a murder mystery named *Monsieur Verdoux* (1947). But much worse, calls came for him to be deported—thrown out of the United States. People suspected him of being a communist.

After World War II ended, there was great tension between the United States and the Soviet Union. They were both superpowers—the only nations capable of dropping a nuclear bomb. Although there were no actual battles, the period became known as the Cold War.

In the United States, panic spread that communists were working in secret within the country to gain power. The US government held hearings of anyone suspected of "un-American activities." (That meant being a communist.) The hearings became a witch hunt. People lost their jobs and found it impossible to get other work. People in the Hollywood film industry were often victims.

But why was Charlie Chaplin a target? For one thing, many thought his political views were too radical. Also, he'd never become a US citizen. When asked why, he answered, "I am a citizen of the world." Charlie had been through three divorces by this time. Each one was dragged through the press. This damaged Charlie's image, too.

Charlie stated firmly that he was not a communist. Although the FBI put together a file of over two thousand pages on Chaplin, nothing was found against him.

In the middle of all this turmoil, Charlie fell in love with Oona O'Neill. The daughter of the famous playwright Eugene O'Neill, she was an intelligent, beautiful woman. And she adored Charlie. They married in June 1943. After three failed marriages, Charlie had finally found long and lasting love. In time, they had eight children.

In 1952, Charlie sailed for Europe with Oona and their children. They were going to London for the opening of Charlie's third talkie, *Limelight* (1952). (Most American theater owners banned the film.)

After two days at sea, Charlie got word from the US government that he couldn't reenter the country until he had proved himself a loyal citizen. Charlie was angry. His adopted country had turned on him. He decided to leave the United States for good.

The Chaplins roamed Europe awhile, staying in luxury hotels. Then, in 1952, Charlie and Oona bought a beautiful estate in Switzerland. There were sweeping views of the Swiss Alps and sparkling Lake Geneva. Charlie happily spent his last twenty-five years there. The family lived in grand style. A large staff of servants cared for the nineteen-room mansion, built in the 1700s. Groundskeepers and gardeners tended the thirty-five acre estate.

In Switzerland, Charlie kept busy. He wrote original music for many of his silent movies. That made him the only moviemaker ever to write, act, direct, cast, produce, and compose music for his own films. He also made his last two films, *A King in New York* (1957) and *A Countess from Hong Kong* (1967). Neither one was as popular as his earlier films.

At this late stage in life, Charlie's family life was happier than before. His youngest son was born when Charlie was seventy-three. His grown sons, Charles Jr. and Sydney, also came for visits. Charlie loved sharing his old movies with his kids in the mansion's large viewing room. No one laughed harder than Charlie.

Chapter 11

Final Bow

On walks in the Swiss hills, Charlie thought back on his long and full life. In 1964, he put it all down on paper: from painful days at the workhouse to the glory days of the Chaplin craze. The once-wordless star wrote five hundred pages. *My Autobiography* was translated into many languages and became a best seller around the world.

Now Charlie's curly hair was stark white. He kept fit by swimming and playing tennis. He played soccer on the front lawn with his kids. Finally, in his seventies, his graceful body began to break down. A cane, his old famous prop, now helped him walk.

By this time, feelings toward Charlie in the United

States had softened. The old fear of suspected communists had faded. Film historians were praising Charlie's pioneering role in movies. His comedies were timeless, they realized. "Who was the greatest actor in movie history?" a 1995 survey asked film critics. They voted Charlie Chaplin number one.

In 1972, he was given a special Academy Award. It was for his part in "making motion pictures the art form of the 20 century."

To receive his special Oscar, Charlie flew to America. It was the first time he'd been in the United States in twenty years. His first stop was New York City, for a screening of *The Kid*.

Then it was on to Hollywood. When he saw Jackie Coogan, his young sidekick from *The Kid*, Charlie burst into tears. The memory of the good old days in silent film flooded back.

Charlie felt nervous about how the audience at the Oscars would respond to him now. But his fears soon fled.

When Charlie came onstage, the audience stood and clapped for twelve minutes. "Oh, you're wonderful, sweet people," he told the audience, tears sliding down his face.

In 1975, Queen Elizabeth II knighted England's native son. The little street waif was now Sir Charlie Chaplin.

Two years later, on Christmas Day, Chaplin died at home in Switzerland, surrounded by his beloved Oona and children. It was the final scene in a remarkable life. He was eighty-eight.

The year 2016 marked the one hundredth anniversary of Charlie's amazing rise to stardom. To honor the anniversary, a Chaplin museum opened in Charlie and Oona's Swiss mansion.

Praise for Charlie has come from all corners. But Charlie himself once said, "I am just a little nickel comedian trying to make people laugh."

Timeline of Charlie Chaplin's Life

1889	Charles Spencer Chaplin is born in London on April 16.
1896	Sent to the Hanwell School for Orphans and Destitute Children.
1901	His father, Charles Chaplin Sr., dies of alcohol abuse at thirty-eight.
1903	Performs in *Sherlock Holmes.*
1908	Showman Fred Karno hires Charlie for his pantomime comedy act.
1913	Signs with Keystone Studios.
1914	Invents the Little Tramp character.
1915	Releases The Tramp for Essanay Film Manufacturing Company.
1918	*Shoulder Arms* becomes a smash hit.
1921	*The Kid,* his first feature film, released to rave reviews.
1924	Shooting on *The Gold Rush* (1925) begins.
1931	World premiere of *City Lights*.
1936	*Modern Times*, set in a factory, opens.
1940	*The Great Dictator*, a WWII satire, is released.
1943	Marries Oona O'Neill; they will have eight children.
1952	His US visa is revoked.
	Moves his family to Switzerland.
1972	Receives a special Academy Award.
1975	Queen Elizabeth II knights Charlie.
1977	Dies at home on Christmas Day, at age eighty-eight.

Timeline of the World

1900	Escape artist Harry Houdini performs for first time in London music halls.
1911	Several film studios open in Hollywood, California.
1913	Henry Ford installs the first moving assembly line for mass production of Ford cars.
1917	The United States enters World War I (1914–1918).
1927	*The Jazz Singer* launches the new era of "talking pictures".
1929	First Academy Awards ceremony is held in Hollywood.
1930	England replaces workhouses with aid programs for the poor.
1932	Walt Disney makes his first color film, a cartoon short called *Flowers and Trees*.
1941	The US enters World War II (1939–1945) following the Japanese bombing of Pearl Harbor.
1952	Princess Elizabeth is crowned Queen Elizabeth II of England.
1954	Senator Joseph McCarthy holds public hearings investigating US citizens accused of being communists.
1961	Disney's *101 Dalmatians* becomes a major hit movie.
1963	Martin Luther King Jr. gives his famous "I Have a Dream" speech at the March on Washington for Jobs and Freedom.
1974	Richard Nixon resigns as president of the United States.

Bibliography

Ackroyd, Peter. Charlie Chaplin: A Brief Life. New York: Doubleday, 2014.

Chaplin, Charles. My Autobiography. New York: Simon & Schuster, 1964.

Crowther, Bosley. "Charlie Chaplin Dead at 88: Made the Film an Art Form."

New York Times. December 26, 1977.

Douglas, Ann. "The Most Important People of the Century." The 2010 TIME 100. June 8, 1998.

*Fleischman, Sid. Sir Charlie: Chaplin, the Funniest Man in the World. New York: Greenwillow Books, 2010.

Lynn, Kenneth S. Charlie Chaplin and His Times. New York: Simon & Schuster, 1997.

McCabe, John. Charlie Chaplin. New York: Doubleday, 1978.

Robinson, David. Chaplin: His Life and Art. New York: Da Capo Press, 1994.

*Turk, Ruth. Charlie Chaplin: Genius of the Silent Screen. Minneapolis, MN: Lerner Publications, 2000.

Vance, Jeffrey. Chaplin: Genius of the Cinema. New York: Abrams, 2003.

*Books for young readers